Lila and Andy learn about

Engineering

A Guide to Engineering as a Career

By
Kenneth Adams

Book Cover by Kenneth Adams
Illustrations by Kenneth Adams
First Edition 2024

ISBN: 978-1-998552-03-0

Never be afraid to explore.
Even if, sometimes, you
have to do it on your own.

Hi! I'm Andy, and this is my sister Lila. This summer, we're spending time at an awesome resort with Mom and Dad. We just love outdoor activities, especially when the weather is great. Today is a bright and sunny day, so we decided to visit an adventure and water park.

This park is so cool! Just look at those slide supports! They're so thin, but they hold up everything! It reminds me of all the bridges Dad, a Civil Engineer, talks about on our road trips. He said civil engineers have to consider loads and forces when they design structures.

And how do they make sure the water flows just right through all those twisty slides? I bet this park needed lots of different engineers to make everything work well together!

Have you ever wondered what engineers are and what they do to make our lives fun and easy?

Today, we want to share with you some of the different types of engineers. Next time, when you visit a park like this, you can try to identify all the different engineers it took to build.

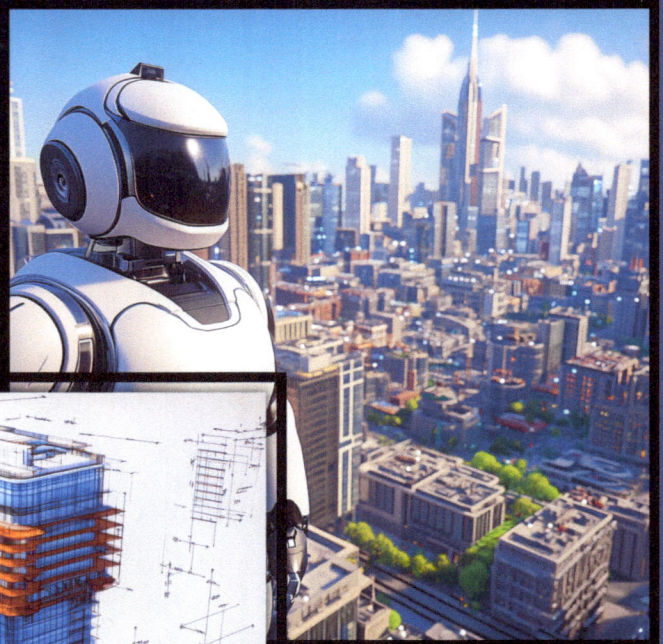

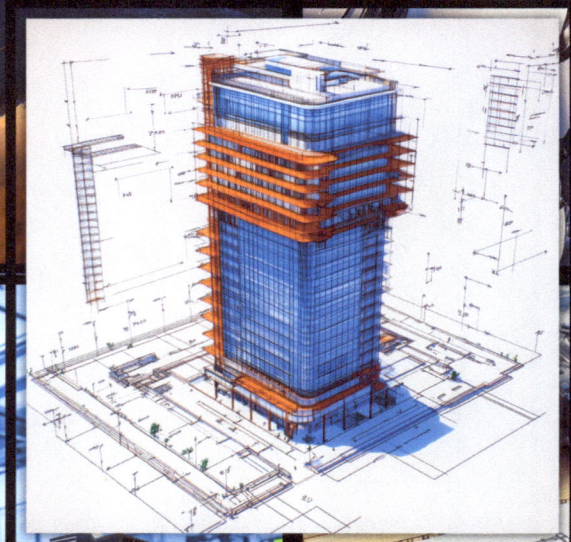

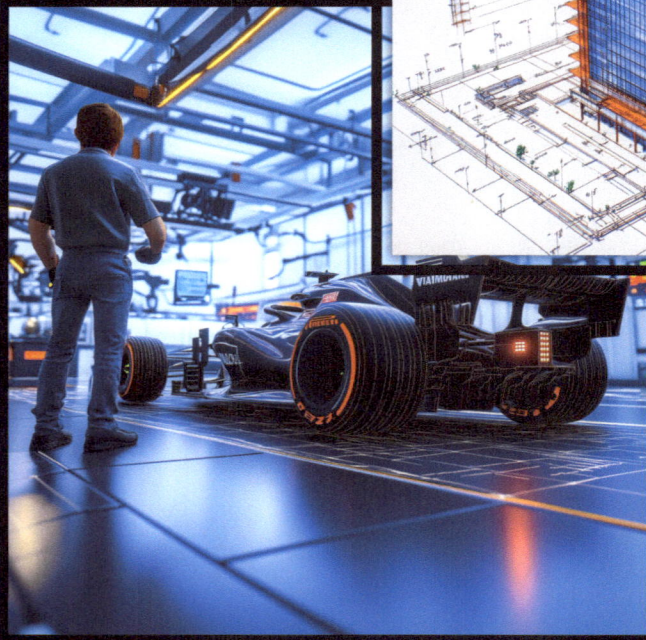

What is Engineering?

Engineering is a type of job, or a profession, that uses math and science to design and create new gadgets, devices, and structures.

Engineers also use their knowledge and experience to come up with ways to improve things that already exist, basically using science to solve problems.

Engineering is everywhere around us. The houses we live in, the cars we ride in, and even the video games we play were all made possible by engineers.

Engineering has been around for a long time, since people started using simple tools like wheels and levers.

Today, engineers work in many different areas to make the things we use every day work better, faster, and safer. They're always finding new ways to solve problems and make our lives easier and more fun.

What are Engineering Disciplines?

Engineering as a profession consists of many different specialties, called disciplines. Imagine engineering disciplines as various flavors of ice cream, each one unique and delicious in its own way!

While each discipline focuses on a specific and unique area of expertise, together, they fit like a giant puzzle to make up the World of Engineering.

The requirements and job responsibilities for each discipline can be very different. This diversity of expertise within the field of engineering makes engineering an exciting profession.

Here are some of the awesome engineering disciplines you could explore.

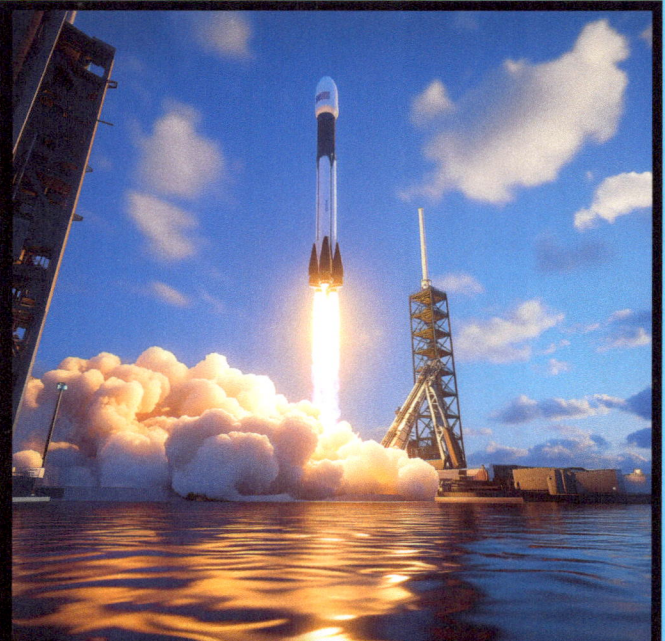

Aeronautical Engineering

Aeronautical engineers are involved with the design, development, and testing of things that fly, like airplanes and rockets. They handle everything from aerodynamics and structural design to propulsion systems. Aeronautical engineers also work on developing unmanned aerial systems, like drones.

Aeronautical engineers need to be great at understanding how things move through the air, and they must have strong problem-solving skills. They work on all kinds of projects, from passenger planes and military jets to space exploration vehicles.

Career opportunities in this field include roles in aviation companies, the government, and aerospace research organizations like NASA. If you dream of designing the next supersonic jet or exploring outer space, aeronautical engineering might be your calling!

Fun fact: Aeronautical engineers helped create the fastest airplane ever, which can fly more than 20 times faster than the speed of sound!

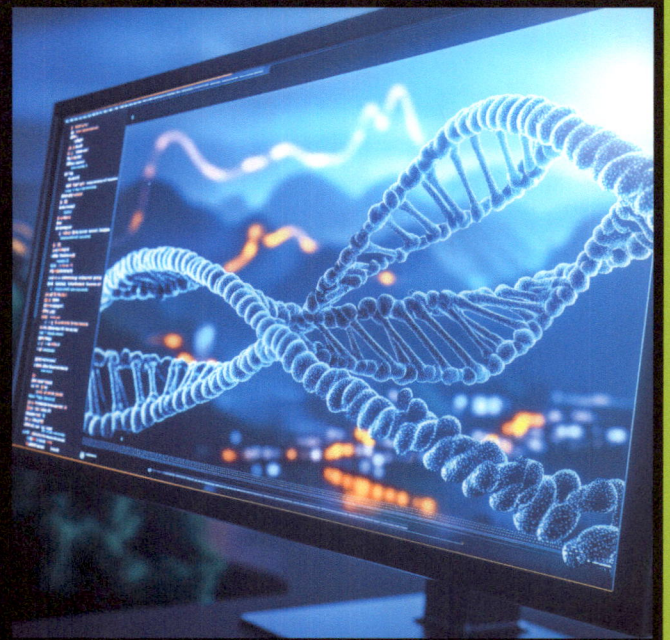

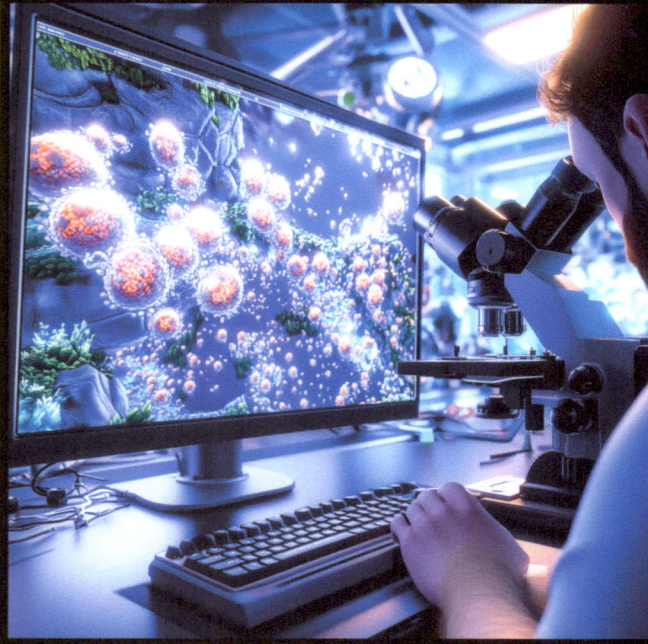

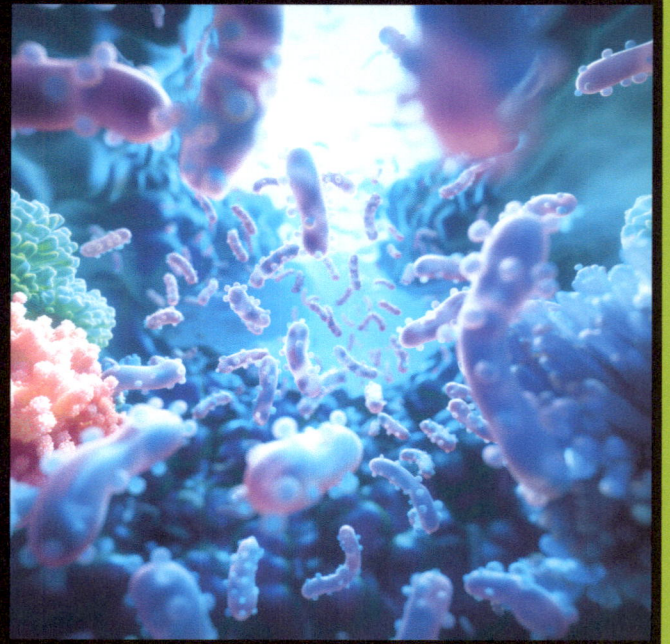

Biological Engineering or Bioengineering

Bioengineers use their engineering skills to work with living things, like plants, animals, and humans. They develop medical devices, create new ways to grow food, and find solutions to environmental problems.

Bioengineers work on cool things like medical devices and even biofuels. That's fuel made from biological products. They need to know a lot about biology and have to work well with other scientists.

Biological Engineers work at medical device companies, pharmaceutical firms, and institutions responsible for biological research. Bioengineering is a great path to explore if you're fascinated by biology and want to use engineering to improve health and sustainability.

Amazing discovery: Bioengineers have created artificial leaves that can produce oxygen, just like real plants do!

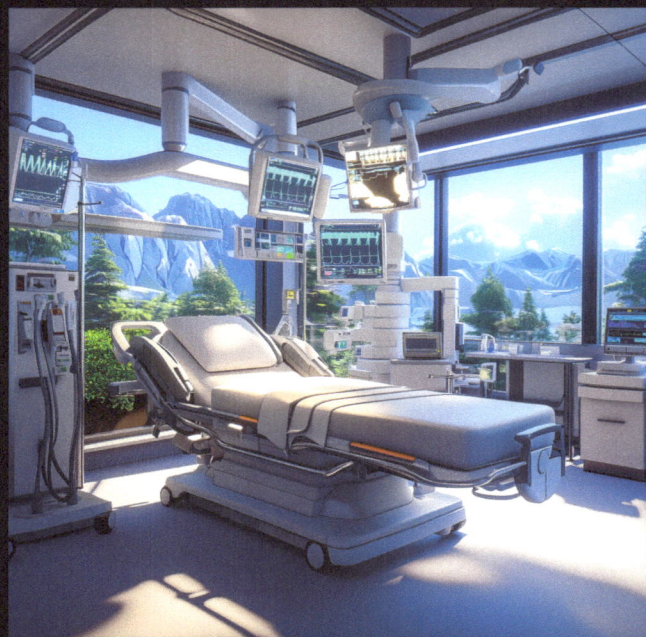

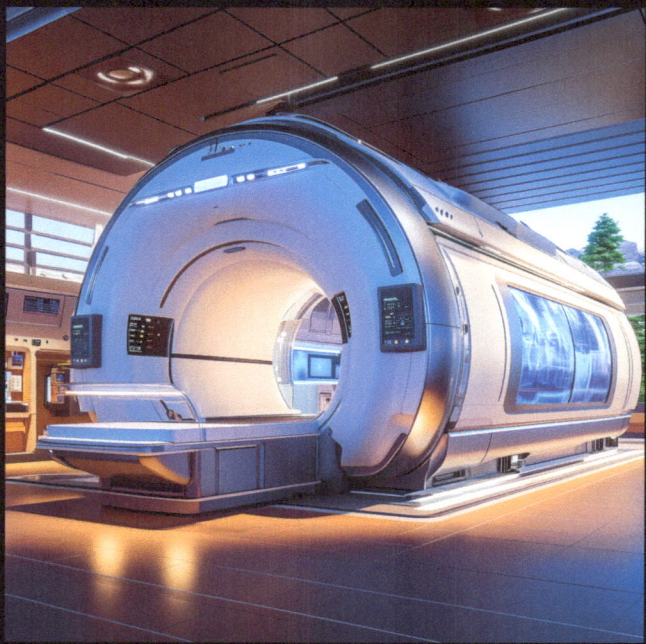

Biomedical Engineering

Biomedical engineers mix engineering with medicine to develop devices and technologies that help doctors and patients. They work on things like medical imaging, artificial limbs, and other tools that improve healthcare.

Biomedical engineers must know about medicine and biology, and they often work closely with doctors and other healthcare professionals.

Career opportunities in this field include roles in medical device companies, hospitals, and research institutions.

If you're interested in medicine and technology and want to make a difference in people's lives, biomedical engineering is an exciting field to consider.

Cool invention: Biomedical engineers have created tiny robots that can swim inside our bodies to deliver medicine exactly where it's needed!

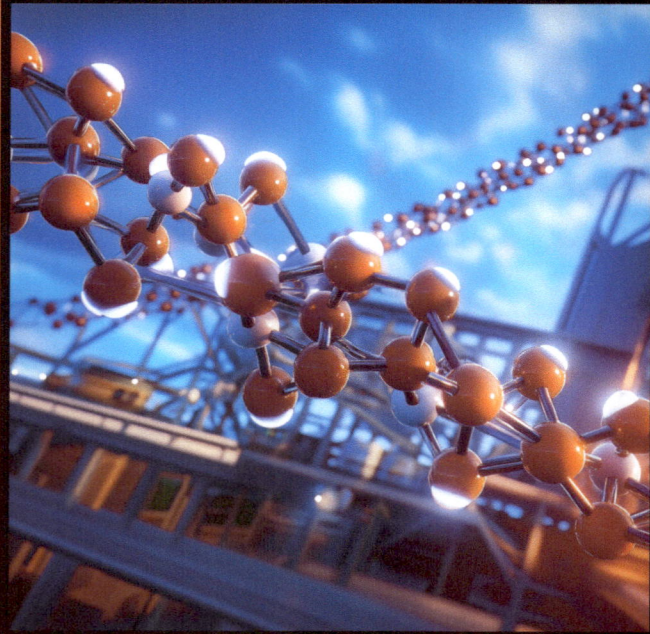
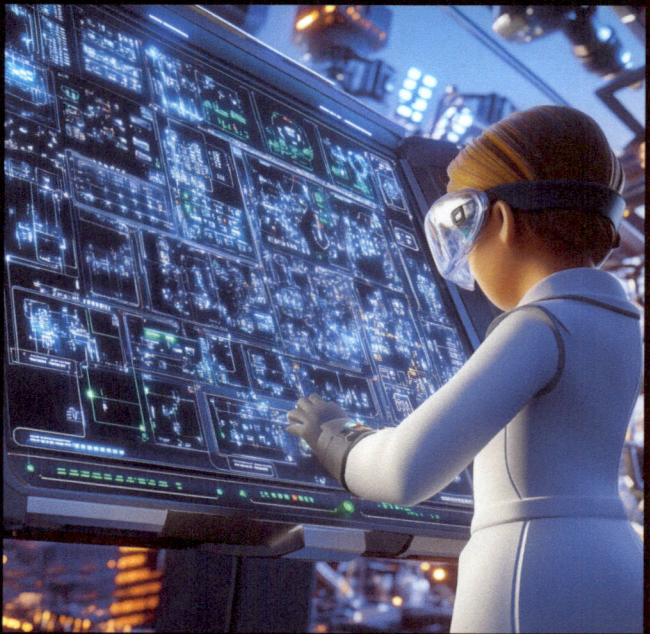

Chemical Engineering

Chemical engineers take raw materials and turn them into useful products. They work with chemicals to create things like medicines, fuels, and even food.

Chemical engineers are problem solvers who need to know how chemical reactions and thermodynamics work. They often work together with other engineers and scientists to develop new materials and products.

They work in various industries, making sure our medicines, fuels, and everyday products are safe and efficient.

If you enjoy chemistry and want to create innovative solutions for a sustainable future, chemical engineering is a fantastic choice.

Did you know? Chemical engineers help make your favorite candies and chocolates taste delicious!

Civil Engineering

Civil engineers shape the communities we live in. They design, build, and maintain everything from bridges and roads to dams, airports, and water systems.

They make sure our buildings remain safe and functional, and they help communities recover from natural disasters like floods, wildfires, or earthquakes.

Civil engineers must be good at project management, structural analysis, and materials science, and they often work closely with architects and construction teams to bring new projects to life.

As a civil engineer, you can follow many different career paths, including working for the government or with private engineering consultancies and construction firms. If you're interested in building and improving our communities, civil engineering is a rewarding path to follow.

Impressive fact: Civil engineers built the world's tallest building, the Burj Khalifa in Dubai, which is over 828 meters, or 2,716 feet, tall!

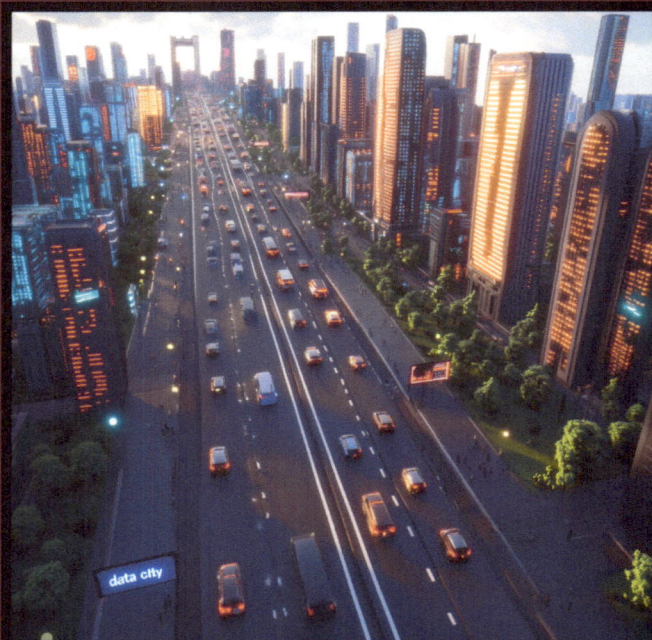

Computer Engineering

Computer engineers are the architects of the digital world. They design and develop hardware and software, working on everything from computers and operating systems to networks.

Computer engineers need strong programming skills and a deep understanding of how computers work. They also work on cutting-edge technologies like artificial intelligence and cybersecurity.

Career opportunities in this field are diverse, ranging from hardware design and software development to systems engineering, IT support, and network administration.

If you love computers and want to be at the forefront of technological advancements, computer engineering is a great field to explore.

Amazing achievement: Computer engineers helped create supercomputers that can perform more calculations in one second than a person could do in millions of years!

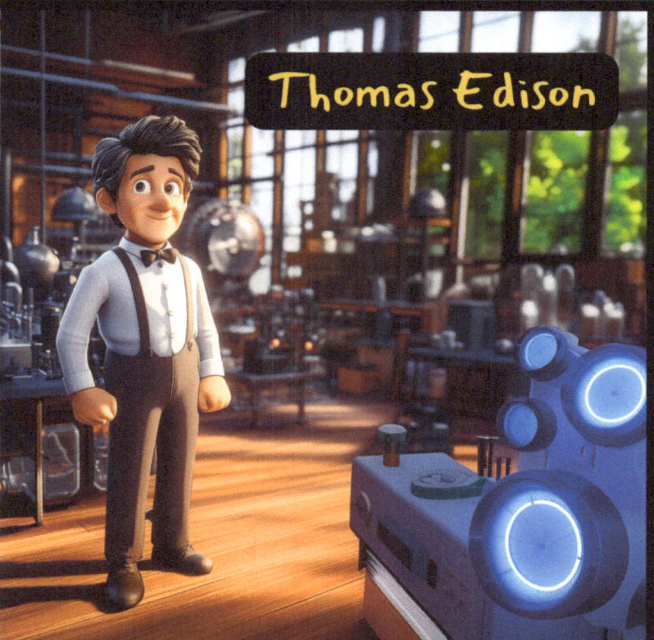

Thomas Edison

Electrical Engineering

Electrical engineers work with electricity. They design and develop electrical systems and components, from power generation and distribution to motors and communication systems.

They play an important role in making sure our electrical infrastructure remains stable, and are at the forefront of developing new technologies such as electric vehicles.

Electrical engineers need to be good at analyzing problems and designing circuits. They work in fields like telecommunications, renewable energy, and electronics, always finding new ways to power our world.

If you're fascinated by electricity and want to work on innovative technologies like electric cars, electrical engineering is a perfect fit.

Cool invention: Electrical engineers have created wireless charging pads that can charge your devices without any cables!

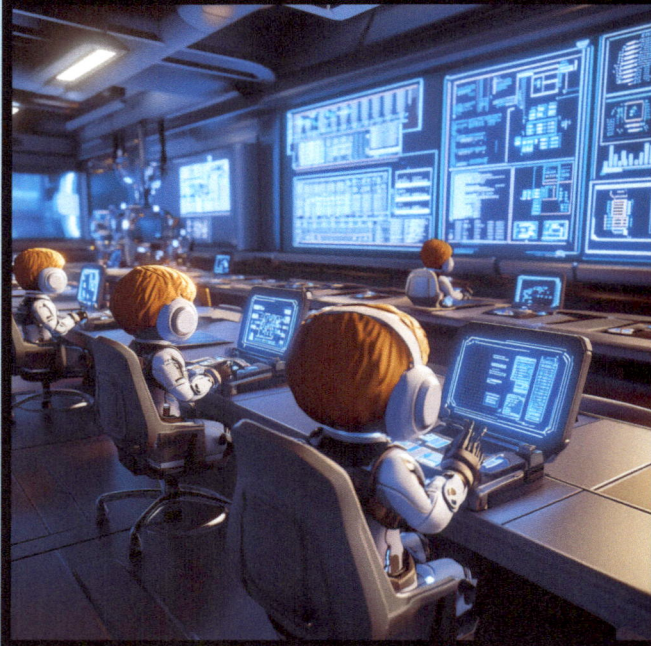

Electronic Engineering

Electronic engineers focus on designing electronic circuits and devices, like the gadgets you use daily. They create everything from smartphones and TVs to medical equipment and industrial automation systems.

These engineers are at the forefront of creating new technology and need to know a lot about circuit design and embedded systems. They often work together with other engineers and designers to develop cutting-edge products.

Career opportunities in this field include roles in sectors such as robotics, communication systems, and consumer electronics.

If you're passionate about electronics and want to design the gadgets of the future, electronic engineering is an exciting field to consider.

Fascinating fact: Electronic engineers helped create flexible displays that can bend and fold without breaking!

Environmental Engineering

Environmental engineers are the guardians of our planet. They create solutions to protect our planet, by solving environmental issues like pollution control, waste management, and water treatment.

Environmental engineers need to know about environmental science and chemistry, and they play a big role in making sure human activities don't harm the Earth.

Environmental engineers work in consulting firms, government agencies, and industries focused on sustainability.

If you care about the environment and want to make a positive impact, environmental engineering is a great way to use your skills for good.

Green innovation: Environmental engineers have designed special floating barriers that can clean up plastic waste from our oceans!

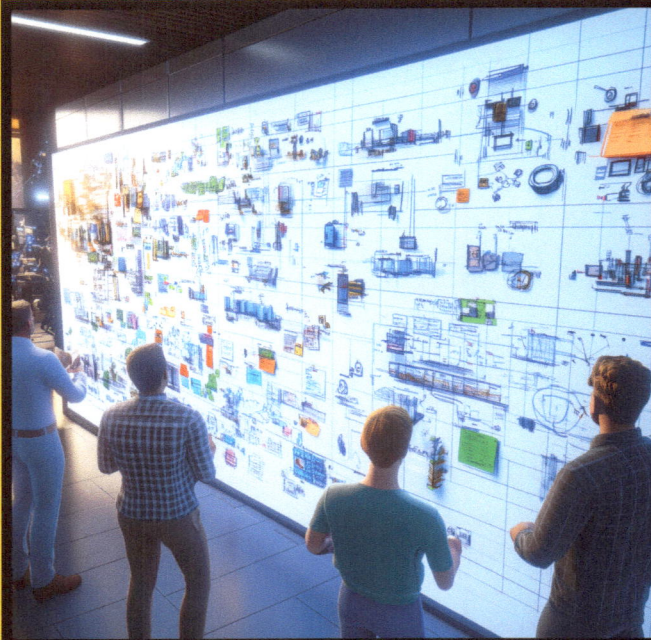

Industrial Engineering

Industrial engineers make systems and processes work better. They analyze data and find ways to improve efficiency, productivity, and quality.

Industrial engineers work on projects to reduce waste, cut costs, and make things run more smoothly. They are experts in process mapping and quality control.

Industrial engineers work in industries like manufacturing, healthcare, logistics, and consulting.

If you're a problem solver who loves to make things work better, industrial engineering is a great option.

Interesting application: Industrial engineers help design theme parks to make sure people can enjoy the most rides with the shortest waiting times!

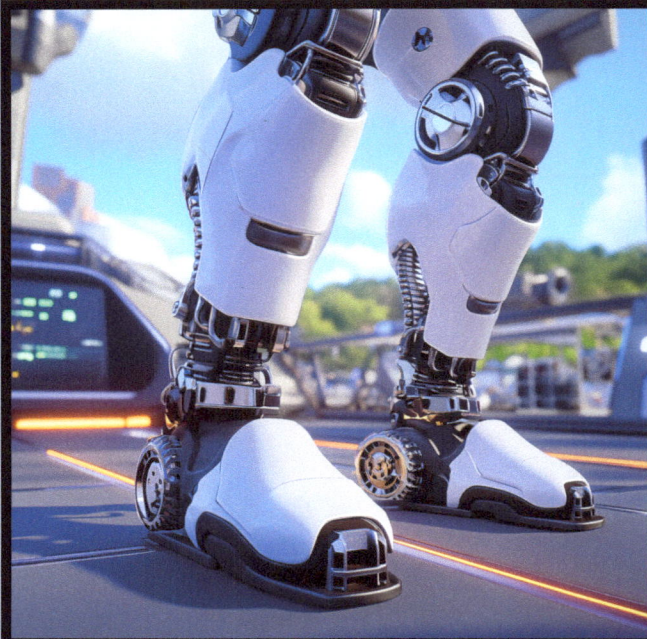

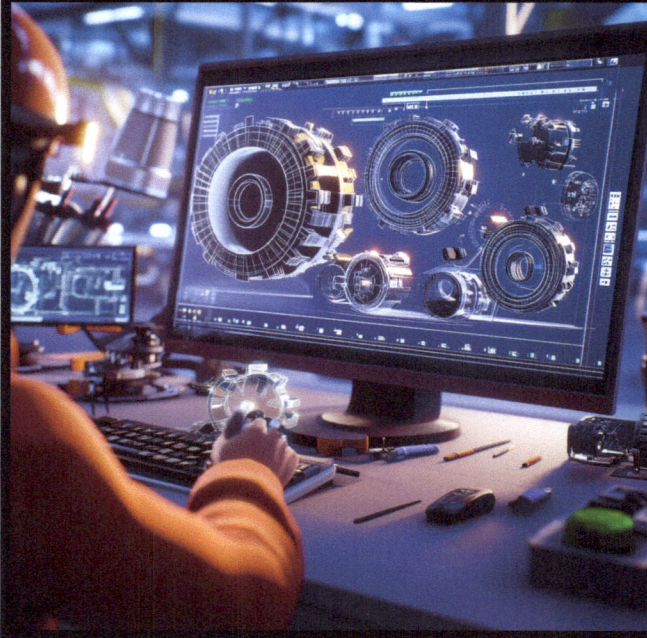

Mechanical Engineering

Mechanical engineers design and build machines, engines, and other mechanical systems. They work on everything from cars and airplanes to heating systems and robots.

Mechanical engineers need to understand how things move and how materials behave. They often use computer-aided design (CAD) software to create detailed models and simulations of their designs.

Mechanical engineers work in manufacturing, such as the automotive, aerospace, and energy industries, as well as with governments and private consulting firms.

If you love tinkering with machines and want to create innovative solutions, mechanical engineering is a fantastic choice.

Cool creation: Mechanical engineers have designed robots that can perform delicate surgeries with incredible precision!

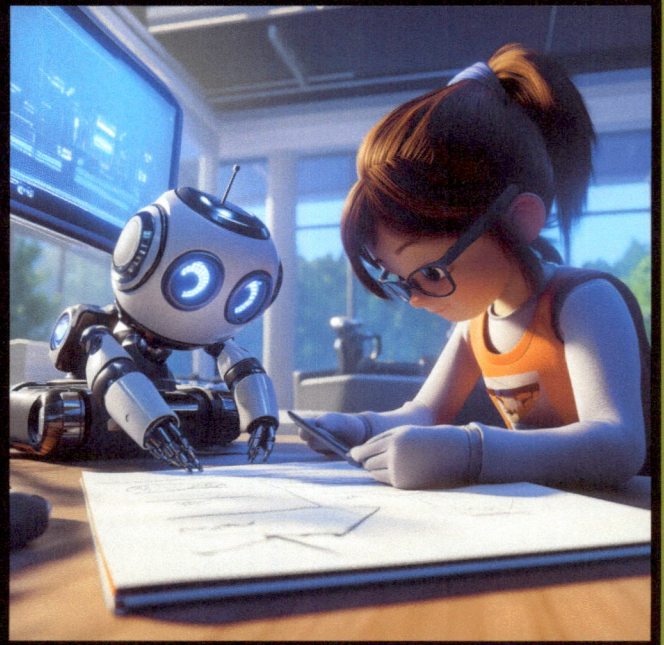

Mechatronic Engineering

Mechatronic engineers combine mechanical, electronic, and computer engineering to create intelligent systems. They work on robotics, automation, and smart devices that make our lives easier and more efficient.

Mechatronic engineers are involved in developing new technologies, and career opportunities in this field include roles in the automotive, aerospace, and consumer electronics industries.

If you're fascinated by robots and want to be part of the next technological revolution, mechatronic engineering is a great field to explore.

Exciting invention: Mechatronic engineers have created self-driving cars that can navigate roads without a human driver!

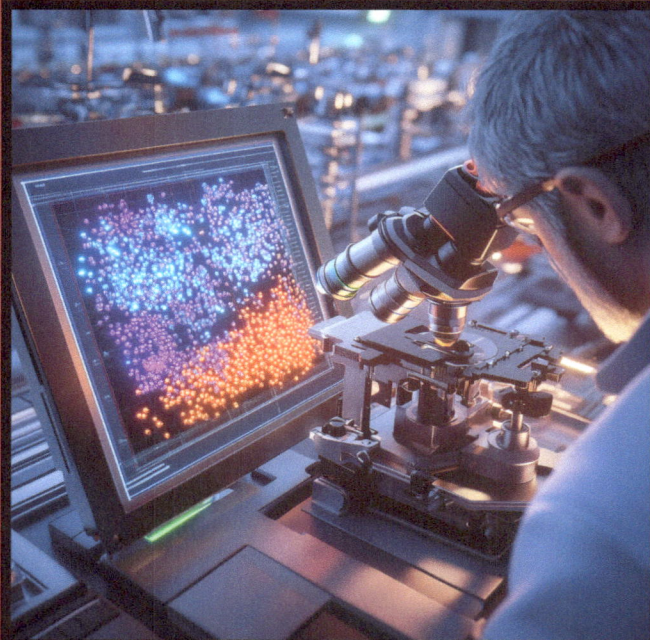

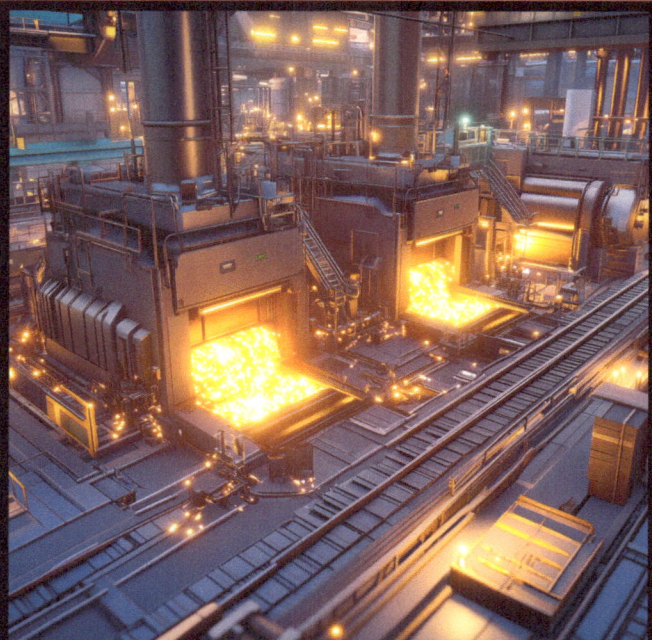

Metallurgical Engineering

Metallurgical engineers study metals and how to make them better. They work on developing new materials and improving existing ones for different uses, like in cars, airplanes, and electronics.

Metallurgical engineers need to understand material science and how to process metals. They focus on material extraction, alloy development, and processing techniques.

Metallurgical engineers work in industries where the performance of metals is important, like aerospace, automotive, manufacturing, and energy. They're always looking for ways to make things lighter, stronger, and more durable.

If you're curious about how metals work and want to help create amazing new materials, metallurgical engineering might be the perfect path for you!

Amazing discovery: Metallurgical engineers have created a metal foam that's strong enough to withstand bullets but light enough to float on water!

Mining Engineering

Mining engineers figure out the best ways to extract valuable minerals from the Earth. They ensure that mining operations are safe, efficient, and environmentally friendly.

They use their knowledge of geology, engineering, and environmental science to plan and oversee the entire mining process, from exploration and excavation to processing and reclamation. Mining engineers are problem solvers who are always looking for ways to improve efficiency, reduce waste, and minimize the impact on the environment.

Career paths in this field include roles in mine management, environmental compliance, and resource exploration. If you're adventurous and want to help uncover the Earth's hidden treasures while protecting our planet, mining engineering could be your perfect fit!

Interesting fact: Mining engineers use special robots to explore dangerous underground areas and keep people safe!

Process Engineering

Process engineers focus on making industrial processes run efficiently and safely. They often work closely with chemical engineers to solve problems and improve production methods.

They're like detectives, always looking for ways to reduce waste, save energy, and make the whole process better for everyone involved.

They work in industries like oil and gas, food production, and manufacturing, always finding ways to make everything run smoothly.

If you're a problem solver who loves to make things work smarter, not harder, process engineering might be the perfect fit for you!

Cool application: Process engineers help design factories that can make thousands of your favorite toys or gadgets every day!

Every engineering field has unique challenges and cool opportunities. No matter what type of engineering you're into, you need to be able to think critically, be creative, and adapt to new things.

Engineers are dreamers and doers who use their imagination and skills to make the world a better place. Whether you want to build new tech, improve infrastructure, or protect the environment, there's an engineering career that's just right for you.